Pip!

Written by Suzannah Ditchburn
Illustrated by Estelle Corke

Collins

Sam pats Pip.

Pip

Dad pats Pip.

pat

Tip it in.

tin

Pip tip tips it.

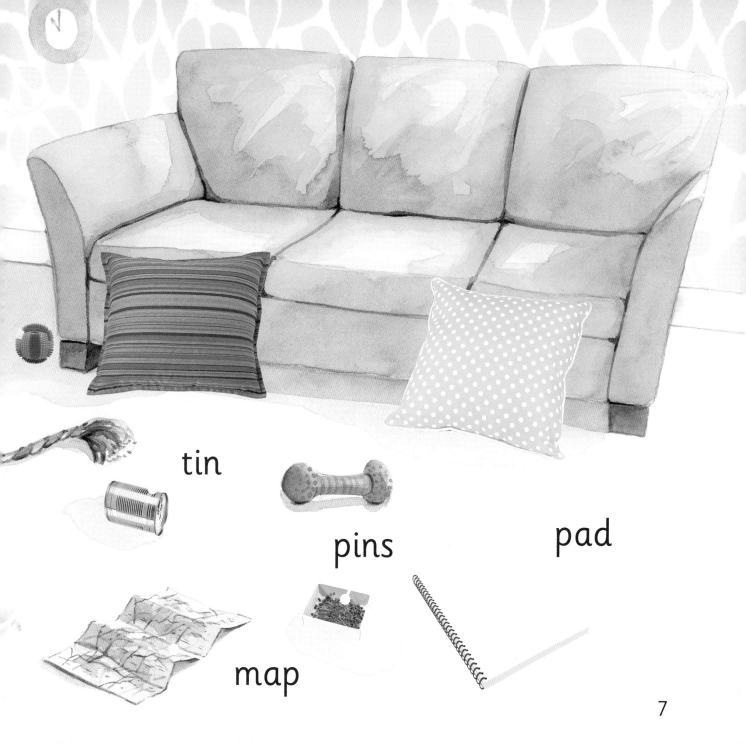

tin

pins

pad

map

Pip sits.

pat pat

8

Pip dips. Pip tips.

Sam sips. Dad sips.

Pip naps.

Dad naps. Sam naps.

/m/

14

15

After reading

Letters and Sounds: Phase 2

Word count: 48

Focus phonemes: /s/ /a/ /t/ /p/ /i/ /n/ /m/ /d/

Curriculum links: Understanding the World

Early learning goals: Reading: use phonic knowledge to decode regular words and read them aloud accurately; demonstrate understanding when talking with others about what they have read

Developing fluency

- Your child may enjoy hearing you read the book.
- Take turns to read a page aloud to each other. Do not forget to read the labels and speech bubbles, too.

Phonic practice

- Turn to pages 6 and 7. Ask your child to find, point to and read words that end with the sound /p/. (*Pip, tip, map*)
- Repeat for:

  /s/   (*tips, pins*)   (t/i/p/s, p/i/n/s)

  /n/   (*tin*)   (t/i/n)

- Look at the "I spy sounds" pages (14–15) together. How many objects can your child point out that contain the /m/ sound and the /d/ sound? (e.g. *map, pram, man, magazine, money*; *dog, beard, doll, dinosaur*)

Extending vocabulary

- Take turns with your child to point to an object in a picture on one of the pages and ask these questions:
  o What is it? (e.g. *a map, a pair of slippers, a pad*)
  o What can you do with it? (e.g. *map: find a town to visit; slippers: keep your feet warm; pad: write a shopping list*)